Job Seeker's Best Friend
© 2023 by Courtney Miller

Published by
Lulu Enterprises, Inc.3101
Hillsborough St.
Raleigh, NC 27607

ISBN: 978-1-105-31349-3

Cover designed by Jim Lodise of Graficore.

Printed in U.S.A.

9 781105 313493

Table of Contents

Part 1: What is a Resume?

Resume Styles...................................PG. 3-4
Resume Format...............................PG. 4-5
Parts of a Resume...........................PG. 5-6
Optional Resume Sections...............PG. 6-7
Applying Transferable Skills ....PG. 7-8
Resume Action Words.................... PG. 8-16
Resume Writing Tips...................... PG. 17
Common Resume Mistakes............. PG. 17-18

Part II: What Are Different Types of Career-Oriented Writing?

The Chronological Resume..............PG. 20
The Functional Resume..........................PG. 21-22
The Computer Scanned Resume.............PG. 23-24
The Cover Letter.......................................PG. 25 -30
The Letter of Inquiry..............................PG. 31
The Reference Page ....PG. 32
The Letter of Acceptance........................PG. 33
The Letter of Decline ....PG. 34
The Resignation Letter.............................PG. 35
The Thank-You Letter..............................PG. 36

Part III: Tell Me More About the Interview Process...

Types of Interviews......................PG. 38
Interview Attire................................PG. 38-39
Before the Interview........................PG. 40
During the Interview........................PG. 40
Common Interview Questions........PG. 41-43
Questions to Ask the Interviewer.... PG. 43-44
Helpful Interview Tips......................PG. 44

Part IV: Do It Yourself Resume/Applications

Sample Job Application......................PG. 46-55
Chronological Resume Worksheet...........PG. 56-62
Functional Resume Worksheet..............PG. 63-68

PART I:

WHAT IS A RESUME!

What is a Resume?

A resume is a recorded summary of skills and experience relevant to your career field. It showcases your significant accomplishments, and reveals to a potential employer that you are qualified for a chosen job. A resume should be designed to market your knowledge, abilities, and experience.

A resume should not only highlight work experiences but detail noteworthy educational, extracurricular, and volunteer experiences as well. Remember, your resume will be the first impression you make on a potential employer. Your words will initially speak louder than your actions. Your resume must be well written, with all of your strongest attributes emphasized.

There are Three Styles of Resumes:

1) Chronological (*see page* 20): This is the most common resume style currently used. The chronological resume presents your educational and work experience in reverse chronological order (starting with the most recent items first).

This style is best for those just starting out in the work force, and for individuals who have remained in the same profession throughout their professional career.

+ Recruiters and employers prefer the chronological resume style because it provides precise history of your education and work experiences, and it is the easiest resume style to scan.

–The chronological resume style does have negative aspects, however. This resume will reveal to employers: a lack of work experience and disruptions in employment history.

2) Functional/Skills (*see pg. 21-22*): A skills resume combines the abilities you have from a wide variety of job-related experiences, including classroom work, volunteer work, paid work, and extracurricular activities. These skills are then grouped by category in relation to a potential job.

+ The skills resume is the best style choice for you if: you have frequently changed jobs, there are gaps in your employment history, or you are changing professions.

– Some employers dislike functional resumes if they find it difficult to match abilities with actual job titles, dates of experiences, and degrees of responsibility.

3) Computer-Scanned (*see pg. 23-24*)**:** A computer-scanned resume is a print resume that is converted into an electronic copy by a potential employer. Scanned resumes utilize Optical Charter Recognition (OCR) software, and are entered into a keyword searchable database.

To compose a successful scanned resume, it is essential that you research the career industry and job position you are applying for, and make sure that appropriate information is included. Always assure that keywords included in the description are included in your resume as well.

HELPFUL HINTS FOR COMPUTER-SCANNED RESUME COMPOSITION:

- Use acronyms and terms specific to the industry in which you are applying.

- When listing acronyms, it is best to fully spell out the name.

   EXAMPLE: PTCB = Pharmacy Technician Certification Board.

- Remember: misspelled words cannot be discovered in a keyword search.

- You do not need to include a section titled "keywords." Key terms will be located in any part of your resume by a search.

Resume Format

The format of your resume builds structure and makes it easier for an employer to read and follow. There are certain guidelines that must be followed to assure that your resume is as reader-friendly as possible.

- Utilize bullet points instead of using paragraph form.

- Assure that all of your information is organized clearly so that it can quickly be comprehended by the reader.

   QUICK FACT: *The average resume is generally only scanned by the employer for 20 seconds!*

- Categories should be arranged in order of importance.

- Use 11-12pt. font.

- A resume should be limited to one page if possible. You should always be as concise as possible while including all relevant information. The one page limit may be exceeded if you have several years of related experience.

- Draw attention to certain details by using **bold** font. Job titles and college majors are commonly bolded.

- Format consistency is key.

    EXAMPLE: Abbreviate ALL of your months, not just some of them. (If you start your resume using "Dec." use this abbreviation throughout.)

Parts of a Resume

Although there are different resume styles and formats, each resume will typically include six subject areas.

Heading: The heading or "header" contains your basic contact information, including full name, address (permanent and current), email address, home phone and cell phone numbers. Your name should be in **bold** and **14-16 pt.** font. Be sure that the e-mail address you include is suitable for professional use.

EXAMPLE: Don't use personal e-mail addresses such as "hotgirl56@wildthang.com."

Summary statement: This section is similar to an objective statement, but instead of stating your career goals, provide a brief summary of your relevant experience and qualifications. *It's important to remember that the content of your resume should be tailored to the specific job are applying for.*

General objectives are acceptable, but not desired. If a general objective is included, assure that you highlight what qualities you can offer the employer. If you are a student applying for an internship, mention when you are available for the program (Spring Semester, Summer Semester, etc.).

Education: Recent graduates should list education details near the top of the resume. All significant training, education, and certificates should be noted. List schools attended, degrees awarded, program/major, and year of completion/graduation. Education should always be listed in reverse chronological order, beginning with the most recent first.

HELPFUL HINT: Grade Point Average (G.P.A.) should only be listed if it is 3.0 or hher.

Experience: Both volunteer and paid experiences should be listed in this section of the resume. List your experience in reverse chronological order; begin with your current job, and conclude with the job that is least recent.

If you have extensive work experience not related to your current field, you can divide this category into "Related Experience," and "Work Experience." The "Related Experience" section should include all of your past experiences related to your present career field, and the job you are currently seeking. This category should be placed near the top of the resume. The "Work Experience" section should include experience not related to your present profession, and be placed below "Related Experiences."

Computer Skills: Your knowledge of certain software and computer systems that will assist you in the job you are applying for should be listed here.

EXAMPLE: Proficiency in Windows XP, PowerPoint, Microsoft Excel

Activities/Honors: Any activities or honors that relate to your career field and can demonstrate your abilities should be included in this section. Activities and Honors can be combined together or stand alone.

> **EXAMPLE:** Student Intern, Rite Aid Pharmacy, 2006
> Top 10 Pharm Tech Student Award, 2006
> Nominee, Pharm Tech University Top 75 Student Program, 2005

Optional Resume Sections

Depending on your career field, and the job position you are seeking, optional sections may be added to your resume. Categories include:

Course Highlights: If you are applying for an internship, a section for course highlights can be added. Courses that are most directly related to the type of work you will be doing in the internship should be listed. If you are a graduate seeking a full-time job in a career field not directly related to your major, you should include classes in relation to the type of job you are seeking.

Leadership: If you have attended any leadership conferences or meetings, or have been in charge of any volunteer projects, include the details in this section.

Languages: If you are fluent in more than one language, list the languages in this category.

International Experience: If you have spent a significant amount of time overseas, or have studied abroad, list your experience in this section.

Applying Transferable Skills

Transferable skills are abilities that transfer from one job to another. These are skills that are learned in past job experiences that can be utilized in future jobs.

Transferable skills are valuable because they can be used in a variety of work-related settings. Customer service, managerial, organizational, and communication skills are all transferable abilities that employers search for and are learned in a wide array of jobs. Other transferable skills include:

* Writing
* Planning
* Analyzing
* Estimating
* Conducting research
* Computer skills
* Foreign language skills
* Public speaking
* Creative thinking skills
* Decision making skills
* Proofreading/Editing skills
* Problem solving skills

When you are creating or revising your resume, you should think in terms of transferable skills. Alter your resume and make it fit the position you are applying for, and then emphasize the abilities that are most relevant to that position. Assemble the job skills and duties you have acquired that are similar to your job interest(s). This will assist you in making connections between the experience you have, and the job you desire.

Once you learn to incorporate the transferable skills you possess into your cover letter and resume, your potential employer will notice your specific qualifications, and realize you have much to offer the company.

EXAMPLE: Let's pretend for a moment that your last working experience was a part-time job at the Burger Kingdom. If you are applying for a management position, note how you developed fresh ideas for the Burger Kingdom, or assisted in new employee training. If you are applying for a position in sales, your bullet points should focus on your customer services skills and selling ability.

HELPFUL HINTS FOR CREATING BULLET POINTS

- Begin with an action verb.

- Give an accurate description of your job responsibilities. Emphasize the duties that highlight your transferable skills.

- Who are you currently assisting in your job description, and what individuals have you assisted in the past?

  EXAMPLE: Co-workers, management, customers, clients, etc.

- Use numbers to show your success rate.

  EXAMPLE: The number of customers assisted, number of times you completed a task, etc...

- Discuss how your efforts have helped to improve the organization as a whole.

Resume Action Words

Resume action words are verbs that are used to accentuate your skills, experiences, and accomplishments. These verbs often replace passive resume phrases such as "duties included," and "responsible for" with animated action words.

If your resume is electronically scanned by a potential employer, the scanner will often become aware of the action words. These dynamic verbs also influence the reader to pay more attention to your resume. The following pages are lists of effective action verbs that describe skills employers are searching for in an employee. Use these lists to help you gather ideas for abilities you can include on your resume.

Common Action Verbs

Analytical/Research Skills		
Analyzed	Detected	Monitored
Assessed	Diagnosed	Recognized
Classified	Evaluated	Refined
Collected	Examined	Researched
Conducted	Extracted	Reviewed
Completed	Explored	Studied
Correlated	Identified	Summarized
Compared	Inspected	Surveyed
Controlled	Interpreted	Synthesized
Corrected	Interviewed	Systemized
Critiqued	Investigated	Theorized
Deciphered	Measured	Transformed

Communication Skills		
Addressed	Formulated	Suggested
Adapted	Greeted	Summarized
Arbitrated	Influenced	Surveyed
Authored	Interpreted	Translated
Briefed	Mediated	Welcomed
Clarified	Persuaded	Wrote
Collaborated	Presented	
Communicated	Promoted	
Consented	Publicized	
Cooperated	Reconciled	
Corresponded	Recruited	
Critiqued	Referred	
Deliberated	Related	
Developed	Reported	
Directed	Represented	
Elicited	Solicited	
Enlisted	Spoke	

Creative Skills		
Acted	Fashioned	Improvised
Brainstormed	Founded	Launched
Conceptualized	Formulated	Originated
Conceived	Generated	Performed
Created	Illustrated	Pioneered
Customized	Initiated	Planned
Developed	Innovated	Polished
Directed	Inspired	Renovated
Drafted	Instituted	Revitalized
Dramatized	Integrated	Shaped
Established	Introduced	Uncovered

Financial/Quantitative Skills		
Accounted for	Counted	Planned
Administered	Dispersed	Profited
Allocated	Earned	Projected
Appraised	Enumerated	Purchased
Approximated	Estimated	Qualified
Audited	Figured	Raised
Balanced	Financed	Reconciled
Boosted	Forecasted	Recorded
Budgeted	Grew	Reduced
Calculated	Grossed	Summarized
Certified	Increased	Tabulated
Checked	Input	Targeted
Compiled	Inventoried	Totaled
Compounded	Managed	Tracked
Computed	Marketed	Transacted
Consolidated	Maximized	
Conserved	Minimized	
Converted	Multiplied	

Helping Skills		
Accommodated	Eased	Mobilized
Advised	Educated	Preferred
Aided	Enabled	Prescribed
Alleviated	Endorsed	Protected
Assessed	Enhanced	Provided
Assisted	Enriched	Relieved
Bolstered	Expedited	Rescued
Clarified	Facilitated	Represented
Coached	Familiarized	Tailored
Counseled	Helped	
Demonstrated	Intercepted	
Diagnosed	Listened	

Management Skills		
Accelerated	Developed	Managed
Administrated	Directed	Motivated
Anticipated	Elected	Observed
Appointed	Evaluated	Organized
Approved	Employed	Oversaw
Assigned	Enlisted	Planned
Assumed	Envisioned	Prepared
Attained	Established	Prioritized
Authorized	Executed	Produced
Caused	Exercised	Prohibited
Changed	Forecasted	Regulated
Conducted	Identified	Reinforced
Contracted	Improved	Reviewed
Commissioned	Influenced	Revised
Consolidated	Initiated	Secured
Coordinated	Increased	Scheduled
Delegated	Handled	Strategized
Designated	Hired	Strengthened
Determined	Led	Supervised

Problem Solving Skills		
Alleviated	Recommended	Satisfied
Debugged	Remedied	Solved
Engineered	Repaired	Suggested
Formulated	Revitalized	
Bugged	Revived	

Teaching Skills		
Adapted	Fostered	Persuaded
Advised	Guided	Presented
Clarified	Graded	Routed
Coached	Illustrated	Set goals
Demonstrated	Informed	Stimulated
Educated	Initiated	Theorized
Enabled	Instructed	Tested
Encouraged	Mentored	Trained
Explained	Modeled	Tutored
Facilitated	Motivated	

Technical Skills		
Assembled	Labored	Programmed
Built	Logged	Proofed
Constructed	Maintained	Remodeled
Designed	Mapped out	Repaired
Engineered	Merchandised	Shipped
Edited	Operated	Solved
Fabricated	Overhauled	Stocked
Installed	Performed	Taught
Inspected	Processed	

Resume Writing Tips

- Use an easily readable font such as Times New Roman.

- Only include relevant work experiences. Elaborate your accomplishments during the interview, not the resume.

- Print the final copy on white or off-white paper. Also, use a laser printer if possible. If you do use an inkjet printer, be sure that the ink is completely dry to prevent smearing.

- Resume categories should be arranged by order of importance.

  EXAMPLE: If customer service skills are your specialty, put this experience near the top of the page.

- Use bulleted sentences to add structure to the body of your resume.

  - Symbols ($, %, #) should always be used. Dollar signs, percentages, and numbers will stand out in the body of a resume.

    EXAMPLE: Increased sales by 23% in a four-state territory.

  - Your strengths should be emphasized. The strongest and most significant points should be included first.

  - Third-party advice is a must. Before sending your resume off, get a neutral opinion from a resume review service or friend. Having your resume subjectively reviewed can provide you with insight on how others perceive your most important marketing tool.

Common Resume Mistakes

There are several reasons why employers may choose to not review your resume. Included below are the most common resume mistakes:

No Cover Letter: Most employers will not review a resume without a cover letter included. Make sure that an appropriate cover letter is attached before sending your resume on its way.

<u>Sloppy Physical Appearance:</u> Poor typing and printing, small or inappropriate fonts, and inconsistent spacing can all add to a sloppy, unprofessional resume appearance. Remember, the resume is the first impression you will make on a potential employer.

<u>Missing Contact Information:</u> It is essential to include contact information such as your name, mailing address, and telephone number. How else do you expect an employer to reach you?

<u>Spelling and Grammatical Errors:</u> Word misuse, poor grammar and spelling, and typographical errors can lead to a disastrous resume. A resume should always be double-checked, and then rechecked by friend, family member, or colleague.

<u>Disorganization:</u> A resume where information is hard to follow and scattered, and where an employer has to search for information is extremely inappropriate. An ideal resume is concise, and easily searchable.

<u>Contains Personal Information:</u> A proper resume should not include personal information such as gender, age, health, height, weight, or marital status.

PART II:

What Are Different Types of Career - Oriented Writing?

The Chronological Resume (Example):

Ian McGee
87 34th. Ave.
Seattle, Washington 48438
Home: (489)494-3839
Cell: (489)389-2289
E-Mail: ianmac@gmail.com

Summary Statement:
Highly skilled and detail-oriented Laboratory Technician with five years of experience in conducting a wide range of laboratory tests and experiments. Proficient in operating and maintaining laboratory equipment, analyzing and interpreting data, and documenting results in accordance with established protocols. Strong understanding of laboratory safety procedures and regulations. Demonstrated ability to work independently and collaboratively in a fast-paced environment. Possesses a Bachelor's degree in Biology and certified in Good Laboratory Practices (GLP).

Professional Experience:

March 2005-Present, CBCC USA, Seattle, Washington
Clinical Laboratory Technician
- Preparing each specimen for analysis and for shipment and storage
- Providing documentation for quality control. This includes cleaning and maintenance of laboratory equipment.
- Monitoring laboratory inventory and placing orders when needed.
- Responsible for maintaining good laboratory practices.
- Collecting data for analysis reports.

July 1996-February 2005, Medical Inc. Labs, Portland, Oregon
Laboratory Manager
- Responsible for management of 7 employees.
- Management of 3 clinical laboratories.
- Identified and solved departmental problems.
- Conducted trouble shooting and department diagnostics.

Education: Bachelor's degree in Biology and certified in Good Laboratory Practices (GLP). University of Washington, Seattle
September 1994-May 1996

Computer Skills: Proficient in Excel, Word, Publisher
Expert in PowerPoint

The Functional Resume (Example):

Allison Jo Little
333 Willow Lane
Providence, RI 38272
(372)884-8201
ajlittle@gmail.com

Highlights of Qualifications

- Twelve years of extensive experience in the Library Science field.
- Awarded "Librarian of the Year" from the Rhode Island Library Association six consecutive years.
- Exceptional customer service and interpersonal skills; able to develop and maintain relationships with co-workers as well as the public.
- Phenomenal ability to follow electronic media, publishing, and computer trends.

Professional Experience

Supervision/Management
- Supervised extensively used Local Area Network
- Trained all library associates in computer and internet techniques
- Assisted in technical instruction of entire library staff
- Managed widely visited computer lab

Organization
- Compiled book lists, articles, and periodicals of specified topics. Also responsible for material analysis
- Composed contents of computer bookstore
- Collected and prepared materials for usage
- Assisted in development and maintenance of library website

Customer Service
- Examined needs of customers to determine what information should be searched for and obtained, in addition to supplying the materials
- Specialized in reference desk reference assistance and research
- Assisted computer users with various web catalogues and online databases

Employment History

2001-Present	Academic Librarian	Rhode Island Public Library	Providence, RI
1997-2001	Reference Librarian	Plainfield Community Library	Plainfield, NJ
1995-1997	Asst. Librarian	County Library	Alexandria, VA

Education

University of Virginia, Charlottesville, VA

Master of Library Science-**May 1997**

Bachelor of Arts, English; Minor, Computer Science-**May 1996**

Computer Skills

Specialize in numerous Microsoft programs including Word, Excel, Office Suite and Publisher

The Computer Scanned Resume (Example):

Maria Moreno
480 Orange Highway
Cleveland, OH 48269
(412)489-4289
mmoreno@aim.com

Summary Statement:
Results-driven insurance sales representative with over 17 years of experience in the insurance industry. Proven track record of achieving and exceeding sales targets by developing and maintaining strong client relationships. Skilled in identifying customer needs and recommending appropriate insurance policies to meet those needs. Proficient in utilizing CRM software to manage customer interactions and increase customer retention. Excellent communication, negotiation, and problem-solving skills. Certified in insurance sales.

Professional Experience:

2005-Present, ABC Insurance, Jacksonville, FL;

Insurance Account Executive

- Responsible for selling health, life, casualty, and property insurance, as well as other company-related products to customers in North Carolina, South Carolina, Georgia, and Florida.

- Manages a department of 23 administrative and executive personnel; responsible for supporting key executive partners.

- Maintains a comprehensive network of business contacts and referral resources.

- Maintains significant knowledge of rules, regulations, and statistics of each company provided insurance line.

2003-2005, United Insurance, Atlanta, GA;
Insurance Sales Representative

- Provided disability and life insurance to residents of South Carolina and Georgia.

- Supervised and managed a department of 13 employees.

- Responsible for recruiting, interviewing, and training new employees.

- Sustained extensive knowledge of all current insurance industry rules, regulations, and trends.

Education:

University of Georgia, Athens, GA
Bachelor of Science in Business Management-**May 2005**
3.98/4.00 GPA

Computer Skills:

Specialty in Word, Excel, Outlook, Microsoft Teams. Proficient in Power Point.

The Cover Letter

The purpose of a cover letter is to specifically detail the reasons for sending a resume. For example, are you seeking a permanent position or just looking for a summer internship opportunity? The cover letter should also explain how you learned of the position. It is appropriate to mention the name of your reference(s).

It is also essential to provide elements of your background. This includes education, experience, and leadership roles that are relevant to the desired position. Personality traits, communication skills and motivation factors should be included as well.

IMPORTANT POINTS TO REMEMBER:

* It is the job of the cover letter to persuade the employer to read your resume.

* The cover letter is the **FIRST** thing a potential employer sees.

* A resume should **NEVER** be sent without a cover letter.

PARTS OF A COVER LETTER

Header: Contact information should be included at the top of your cover letter. Standard letter format may be used, or you may also use your resume header.

Opening Paragraph: The purpose of the opening paragraph is to grab the attention of the employer. Name the position you are applying for, and establish your knowledge about the position. You should also explain how you learned about the job.

Body: The body of the cover letter should describe why you qualify for the position. The information contained in your resume SHOULD NOT be repeated. The body should be used to elaborate on your resume information. Specific experiences or projects should be included in this section. Paragraph form, bullet form, or a combination of both may be used in the cover letter body.

Closing: The closing section of the cover letter is where you ask the employer for an interview. Include what steps you intend to take next, and follow through with those promises. Contact information should also be included here.

Salary History (*optional*) An employer will occasionally ask for your salary history to gauge how much money you expect to earn. If you are asked for your salary information, this issue should be covered somewhere in the closing paragraph. A salary range should be given, and you should always let the employer know you will negotiate.

TYPES OF COVER LETTERS

Letter of Inquiry: This should be sent when no opening is advertised.

Letter of Application: This is sent along with a resume for a specific position that has been advertised.

Reference Page: This should contain contact information and 3-6 professional references. The reference page should have the same heading as your resume.

Letter of Acceptance: When requested, send as a formal acceptance to a job offer.

Letter of Decline: A letter of decline should be sent when you do not want to accept a job offer.

Letter of Resignation: When you are planning to resign from your present position, send a letter of resignation.

Thank you Letter: A thank you letter should be sent to an employer to express gratitude for a meeting or interview.

Cover Letter Example 1: (in reference to job advertisement)

**_Job Ad_: Leading retail store searching for a qualified pharmacy technician to join their pharmacy team. Must have at least 2 years' experience and great customer service and communication skills. Interested parties should contact Ms. Sharon Brown, Human Resources Manager, CPS Drug to schedule an interview. **_

Melody Anderson
7385 Winters Highway
Columbia, SC 37962
MAnderson@yahoo.com

March 12, 2022

Ms. Sharon Brown
Human Resources Manager
CPS Drug
342 April Street
Greenville, SC 37936

Dear Ms. Brown,

I saw your listing on Indeed.com searching for a qualified pharmacy technician. As a pharmacy technician at Rite Drug Company for six years, I gained indispensable experience in the pharmacy field. I am interested in moving forward in my career, and am extremely interested in obtaining a position in your store.

As a dedicated employee for many years, I have exceptional communication and customer service skills. I can assure you that I would be a valuable asset to your pharmacy team.

Please contact me if you would like to meet with me and further discuss this position. I can be reached on my cell phone, 999-555-0000 to schedule an interview at your convenience. Thank you for your consideration, and I look forward to hearing from you soon.

Sincerely,

Melody Anderson

Enc: cover letter and resume

<u>Cover Letter Example #2:</u> ("cold call" cover letter)

Mark Bender
3827 4th Street Drive
Los Angeles, CA 93829
MBender@gmail.com

February 5, 2019

Jennifer Brady
Human Resources Manager
Dot Com Computer Company
446 Center Street
San Francisco, CA 39372

Dear Ms. Brady,

I am contacting you to inquire about available positions for Computer Tech Specialists in your company, Dot Com Computer.

I have comprehensive knowledge of three computer languages, in addition to exceptional support and sales experience. As a Tech Specialist for five years at WWW Computer Corporation, I was responsible for supervising the main technical support system, both on and off-line. I received a Bachelor of Science degree in Business Administration from UCLA in December of 1999, and will receive my Masters in Computer Science in May of this year.

I am confident that I can become a great asset to the Dot Com Computer team if given the chance. I would greatly appreciate the opportunity to meet with you to further discuss the needs of your company. I will contact you next week to schedule an interview, or you may call me at your convenience, (999)555-3929.

Thank you for your consideration, and I look forward to hearing from you.

Sincerely,

Mark Bender

HELPFUL HINT: If no job opening is advertised, you will need to compose a different cover letter, such as the "letter of inquiry" (see page 31). Your resume should always be enclosed with the letter. It is also advisable to follow your inquiry with a phone call; ask the company if your letter was received, and if they are currently hiring.

Corresponding Via E-Mail

In today's technology driven society, it is common practice to correspond solely through e-mail. There are certain elements that must be considered to compose and send the ideal e-mail to a potential employer.

* Unless requested otherwise, all attachments should be in the Microsoft Word format. It is suggested to test your documents by sending them to family and friends. This will assure that the files open easily on various computers and systems.

* Each file should be named with a document description, as well as your name.

EXAMPLE: bob-jones-coverletter.doc, bob-jones-resume.doc, bob-jones-references.doc

* The job code or job title should be used as the e-mail subject. You may also want to include your name in the subject line.

* An e-mail message is generally used as the cover letter when sending a resume. Unless an additional cover letter is requested, the cover letter can be pasted into the body of the e-mail.

* Your initial correspondence should be brief if an additional cover letter is requested by the employer. Simply state the position you are applying for, and that a cover letter and resume is attached to the e-mail.

* Your e-mail address, greeting and signature line **MUST** be professional. It is ideal to have separate personal and business e-mail accounts.

* When you correspond with an employer, **ALWAYS** be polite and professional.

E-Mail Correspondence Example:

Dear Mr. Connor,

I am extremely interested in applying for the Graphic Design position advertised in *Designers Weekly*. I would greatly appreciate your consideration for this position, and have attached a cover letter and resume. Thank you so much for your time, and I look forward to hearing from you.

Sincerely,

Anna Miller

Attached: cover letter and resume

The Letter of Inquiry (Example):

Karen Jackson
66 Mockingbird Lane
Jersey City, NJ 38927
KJackson@yahoo.com

March 12, 2021
Angelo Kelly, Hiring Manager

4673 Highway 4
Newark, NJ 48934

Dear Mr. Kelly,

I have recently been informed of a job opportunity as a Sales Representative for your company Sales United. I am very interested in this position because of my years of sales experience, and exceptional communication and interpersonal skills.

I am currently employed at ABC Sales Company in Jersey City as a Sales Assistant.

Thank you so much for your consideration, and I look forward to discussing how I can greatly add to the success of ABC Sales Company.

Sincerely,

Karen Jackson

The Reference Page

A reference page can be sent with your resume, or can be given to employers when they ask for references. Ideal references are people who can positively attest to your character, skill, and work ethic. This may include co-workers, clients, teachers, or past supervisors. Individuals included as references should always be asked for permission. Your references should also be sent a copy of your resume, and thank you notes.

The Reference Page Example:

Allison Parker
736 Willow Street
Philadelphia, PA 48297
(479)382-3892
aparker30@yahoo.com

REFERENCES:

Abby Wright

Department Supervisor
123 Auto Sales
435 5th Street
Pittsburgh, PA 42487
(478)489-4047

Timothy Bates

Assistant Manager
Health Aid Pharmacy
325 9th Street Drive
Nashville, TN 73497
(587)389-9023

Jim Starnes
Camp Director
Camp Sunshine
34 High Way
Denver, CO 83947
(282)903-2903

The Letter of Acceptance (Example):

Fiona Hart
836 Shine Street
Fairfield, NJ 83293
FHart@yahoo.com

April 24, 2022

Michael Sampson
ABC Drug
888 Apple Way
Boston, MA 87383

Dear Mr. Sampson,

I am writing to confirm our phone conversation, which took place on April 23, 2020. I am extremely excited to accept ABC Drug's offer to become your newest Pharmacy Technician Manager for a yearly salary of 45,000 and an extensive benefits package. As I have formally resigned from Rite Drug, I will be relocating to the Boston area in the next two weeks. I will be able to give you an exact starting date by Monday.

I would like to thank you again for allowing me to join the team at ABC Drug. If you have any questions, or need additional information, I can be reached at (999)555-3892.

Sincerely,

Fiona Hart

The Letter of Decline (Example):

Marshall Smith
87 West Way
Plainfield, NJ 84730

January 3, 2021

Jay Manchester
Human Resources Manager
All Rite Pharmacy
8470 6th Street
Plainfield, NJ 84730

Dear Mr. Manchester,

I would like to thank you for taking the time to meet with me last Monday.

After careful consideration, however, I must decline your attractive offer for the Pharmacy Technician position. At this point in my career, I have decided that my goals and interests lie elsewhere. Perhaps we will professionally collaborate at another time.

Thank you again, and best of luck in your continued success.

Sincerely,

Marshall Smith

The Letter of Resignation (Example):

Mitch Smith
456 North Main Street
Charlotte, NC 25874

April 13, 2022

James Carter
Human Resources Manager
Carter and Carter Design
8748 7th Street
Atlanta, GA 48730

Dear Mr. Carter,

I am writing to inform you of my resignation, effective April 30th. Although I have enjoyed my job as Art Director, I have accepted another position where I believe my diverse talents can be completely applied.

I would like to thank you for the tremendous experience I have had with Carter and Carter Design. It has been a pleasure to be a part of such an exceptional staff these past 12 years.

I hope that Carter and Carter will continue to flourish. I wish you the best of luck.

Sincerely,

Mitch Smith

The Thank You Letter:

Thank you letters should be sent after any type of meeting. This includes informal interviews, job interviews, and networking opportunities. A letter should be sent to each individual person who spent a significant amount of time with you. When sending a thank you letter, ALWAYS be prompt; your letters should be mailed and/or emailed 24-48 hours after a meeting or interview. A letter can be sent on a NEATLY hand-written thank you card, or as a typed letter.

Marsha Abbott
497 Wandering Lane
Charlottesville, VA 34729
MAbbott@yahoo.com

June 9, 2022

Courtney Anderson, Dept. Manager
Southern Sales
89 Eastern Highway
Richmond, VA 34897

Dear Ms. Anderson,

Thank you so much for meeting with me June 7 to discuss the Sales Manager position. It was a delight to learn more about the position possibilities and significant advancement opportunities available at Southern Sales.

After 12 years of customer service and sales experience, and my exceptional communication skills, I am confident that I could be an asset to your sales team.

Thank you once again for your time and consideration, and I look forward to hearing from you next week.

Sincerely,

Marsha Abbott

PART III:

Tell
Me More
About the Interview
Process

Tell Me More About the Interview Process...

Types of Interviews

Group Interview: In this type of interview, you are a member of a group or team interviewed at the same time.

Panel Interview: You will be questioned by future co-workers or committee members in a panel interview.

Phone/Zoom Interview: If you have found a job that is a long distance from your current location, you will most likely have a phone and/or Zoom interview. Anytime you contact any employer, be prepared to answer interview questions.

Interview During a Meal: Many times, a final interview will be conducted during a meal. This is so the prospective employer can see how you act in public, during a social, dining situation. One of the most stressful interviews, the organization is closely watching how you interact with company representatives. You must also know how to dine in a formal environment, so brush up on your dining etiquette!

Proper Interview Attire

Appearance plays a crucial role in the interview process. There are certain elements that must be taken into consideration when preparing for any interview.

* Attention to detail is a must. Be sure that your hair is neatly groomed and well-trimmed, your dress or suit is ironed, and all buttons are securely sewn.

* Too much perfume or cologne is discouraged.

* An off-color shirt or blouse is preferable interview wear for both men and women.

WOMEN:

* Bright or flashy colors should be left at home. Just say no to hot pink tights or bright red lipstick. Subtle colors are best suited for a job interview.

* Stay away from short skirts and lowcut blouses. Keep makeup subtle.

* Don't over accessorize. Extravagant necklaces, earrings, belts, or rings can be distracting.

* A black suit (skirt or pants) is the safest bet when interviewing. Grays and navy blues are also suitable colors to wear.

MEN:

* Any facial hair should be trimmed or shaved.

* Earrings, hats, or showy neckties should never be worn to an interview.

* A dark suit coat in black, navy blue, or gray is best for an interview. Pair this with matching pants and tie, and a white or light blue dress shirt. Don't forget to shine your shoes!

15- Point System for Proper Interview Attire:

**Each item has a one-point value, in some case two points. **

Point Scale:
Eight points or less: Too underdressed or plain
Nine to fourteen points: Optimal range
Fifteen points or more: Too overdressed or flamboyant

Point System:
Bald head: 1 point
Blonde or Red hair: 1 point
Scarf, bows, ties: 1 point
Purse, briefcase: 1 point
Tie tack, tie bar: 1 point
Each jewelry item: 1 point (pair also count as 1 point)
Eyeglasses: 1 point
Visible eyeglasses or pen case: 1 point
Dress, skirt, pants, jacket, sweater, sports coat, socks, nylons, belt, shoes: 1 point
Blouse, shirt: 1 point
Visible tattoos: 1 to 2 points
Large earrings: 2 points
Large broaches or pins: 2 points
Fancy or oversized belt buckle: 2 points

Before the Interview

Before meeting with your potential employers for an interview, it is a good idea to research both the position you are applying for, as well as the company. To obtain a job description, you can either visit the company website or call. Always bring copies of your resume, your reference page, in addition to a pen and pad of paper. These items should be enclosed in a professional folder or briefcase. You should also make sure that you know the exact location of the office building. You can double check your directions through a print or online map, or through directions from the company website. Remember to give yourself adequate time to drive to your destination.

During the Interview:

The interview process gives you the chance to sell yourself to a potential employer. It is your job to relay to the interviewer why you feel you are the best fit for a certain position. It is key to mention the qualities and skills you possess. You should enter every interview with a clear idea of what you want to accomplish and devise a plan of how to get those points across during the interview process.

Enthusiasm is crucial during an interview. You want to convey your extreme interest in a job without going over the top. Remain sincere; never rave about a company that you have no interest in. To show true passion, you must interview for jobs that excite you and match your interests.

During an interview, it is essential that you pay attention to what the interviewer is saying. If you don't listen well during an interview, that tells the interviewer that you may have the same problem when it comes to the job.

It is also important that YOU keep the interviewer's attention. Basic public speaking rules can easily be applied to any interview environment:

- Always maintain eye contact with the interviewer

- Vary both the tone and tempo of your voice

- Translate all of your nervous energy into enthusiasm for the job

It is also a good idea to try to correspond to the interviewer's energy level. Most individuals will usually hire those similar to themselves.

Common Questions Interviewers Ask

Below are typical questions asked by employers during interviews. Practicing your answers with a friend can be helpful before any interview.

* How would you describe your personality?

* What are some of your strengths and weaknesses?

* What are a few ways you could contribute to our organization?

* What specifically do you do to set standards for employees?

* Do you work best on your own or under supervision?

* Do you work well under pressure?

* Describe the relationship that should exist between a supervisor and his team.

* What things frustrate you the most? How do you deal with these things?

* Please give an example of a situation when you have experienced a conflict with a peer. How was this conflict resolved? What resulted from the situation? Would you have handled the conflict differently now?

* What is more important to you the type of job, or the money?

* Tell me a bit about your scholastic record/achievements.

* What was your major in college? Why did you choose that particular major?

* What were some of your favorite courses? Least favorite? Why?

* What facets of your education/training have prepared you for this position?

* What was the most difficult decision you have made in the last six months?

* Describe one or two of your greatest achievements.

* Have you recently made any presentations? How did you prepare?

* What do you do in your spare time?

* Have you ever quit a job? Why?

* Why do you want to leave your current job?

* Why did you want to interview with our company?

* Give examples of situations where you have had multiple priorities. What were these situations, and what was the final result?

* Where do you see yourself in five years? Ten years?

* Would you be willing to work on Holidays and some weekends?

* Why do you feel you would be successful in this company?

* Why should we hire you?

** HELPFUL HINT**

Employers are not allowed to ask questions in regard to marital status, age, race, religion, gender, sexual orientation, children, or childcare arrangement. Questions relating to circumstances that are not specific to the job you are interviewing for are considered to be illegal. Illegal questions can be answered 3 ways:

- Answer the question.

- Refuse to answer the question.

- Ask the interviewer to clarify the question.

When asked an inappropriate question, remain polite and do not be defensive. If the interviewer continues to act in an aggressive manner, you may want to re-evaluate your desire to work for the company.

When Questioning an Interviewer

* You should only ask questions which you want an answer. Some individuals only ask certain questions hoping to impress the potential employer.

* You should never waste the time of the interviewer, as they will eventually uncover your charade.

* Never ask questions that can easily be answered through the job description or company website.

* Wait until you have been offered the job before asking questions about salary and other benefits.

If you are already experienced in the field, and you need to know if this position falls within your salary range, it is acceptable to ask however.

Common Questions to Ask an Interviewer:

Below are common questions YOU can ask a potential employer. Review these questions before an upcoming interview, or print out a copy and carry it along.

* Describe your company's work environment.

* What are the responsibilities of this position?

* What are some department goals for the current year?

* Explain to me the expectations you have in the first three to six months for your new hires.

* What are some of the more challenging elements of this position?

* What characteristics are you searching for in your new hires?

* What is a realistic time frame for promotion and advancement?

* Detail typical first year assignments associated with this job.

* Describe to me the company's performance evaluation methods.

* What traits must an individual have to succeed in this organization?

* Does your company support continuing education?

* Is the policy of promotion from within the company encouraged by management?

* I read in your brochure that your training is composed of three, three-month cycles. How is the employee's performance evaluated during each training session?

* What makes your organization different from others?

* What are your company's strengths and weaknesses?

* What is the next step I need to take to become a part of your team?

* I am very interested in this position! Could I have a 30-day trial period to prove myself to you?

Helpful Interview Tips

* Always arrive at least fifteen minutes before the interview. This will assure that your arrival is not hindered by traffic or other delays. It will also decrease your stress level.

* A pen and pad of paper are essential items to bring with you to any interview (it is suggested that you take notes).

* When you greet your interviewer, extend a firm handshake and flash a friendly smile. Greet your interviewer by name; use the formal "Mr." or "Ms." unless you are told otherwise.

* Wait for the interviewer to sit down before you seat yourself.

* No smoking or gum chewing!

* Maintain good posture and eye contact.

* If you are asked a difficult question, take a few seconds before responding. Really listen to what the interviewer is saying.

* You should always end the interview positively. Express your interest in the position and relay why you think you are the best candidate. Remember to thank the interviewer for his or her consideration and time.

PART IV:

DO IT YOURSELF: JOB APPLICATION AND RESUME WORKSHEETS

Sample Job Application

*Below is an **actual** job application. This can be used for practice, reference, or filled out in advance, and taken to a job interview.*

Name: (last, first, middle)_____

Date: _____

Street Address: _____

City, State, Zip: _____

Home Phone: (   )-_____-_____

Business Phone: (   )-_____-_____

Email: _____

Social Security Number: _____-_____-_____

Are you over 18 years of age? _____Yes _____ No

Are you legally eligible to work in the United States? _____Yes _____ No

Have you ever been convicted of a crime (misdemeanor or felony) other than a basic traffic violation? (*NOTE: This information will not automatically disqualify you from employment, but will be used for job placement and hiring.*) _____ Yes _____ No

If your answer is yes, please provide a brief explanation of the situation:

_____

_____

_____

Position Desired: _____Full Time_____Part-Time (check appropriate)

Have you ever applied for employment with us previously? _____Yes _____ No

If your answer is yes, please provide the year of application and location:

_____

_____

Desired yearly salary: _____

When will you be available to begin work with our company?

_____

If asked, will you be able to work overtime with our company?

_____

Please provide the referral source to this company:

_____Self _____Current Employee _____College Recruiter_____ Other

Education

HIGH SCHOOL

Name and Location of High School:

_____

Number of Years Completed:

_____

Did You Graduate? _____Yes _____ No

Degree, Certificate or Diploma:

_____

COLLEGE

Name and Location of School:

_____

Major(s): _____

Number of Years Completed:

_____ __

Did You Graduate? _____ Yes _____No

Degree, Certificate or Diploma:

_____

Name and Location of School:

_____

Major(s): _____

Number of Years Completed:
_____

Did You Graduate? _____ Yes _____No

Degree, Certificate or Diploma:

_____

BUSINESS, TRADE, TECHNICAL, ETC.

Name and Location of School:

_____

Major(s): _____

Number of Years Completed:

_____

Did You Graduate? _____ Yes _____ No

Degree, Certificate or Diploma:

_____

Computer and Software Skills

What computer systems are you familiar with, and have you worked with previously? (**EXAMPLE:** MAC, PC, etc.)

_____

_____

_____

What software applications are you most familiar with? (**EXAMPLE:** Microsoft Word, Excel, etc.)

_____

_____

What other technology background and knowledge do you possess?

_____

_____

_____

Employment Experience

Please include complete part-time and full-time employment record. Also, list your last four employers, listing your most recent employers first.

Employer Name:

_____

Telephone: (   ) _____-_____

Street Address:

_____

City: _____   State: _____   Zip: _____

Dates of Employment: (State, Month, Year) _____

From: _____   To:_____

Supervisor Name:

_____

Hour or Weekly Salary: (Start to Last) _____

Job Title:

_____

Job Description:

_____

_____

Reason for Leaving:

_____

_____

May the Employer be Contacted? _____Yes _____No

Employer Name:

_____

Telephone: (   ) _____-_____

Street Address:

_____

City: _____ State: _____ Zip: _____

Dates of Employment: (State, Month, Year)

From: _____To: _____

Supervisor Name:

_____

Hour or Weekly Salary: (Start to Last)

_____

Job Title:

_____

Job Description:

_____

_____

Reason for Leaving:

_____

_____

May the Employer be Contacted? _____Yes _____No

Employer Name:

_____

Telephone: (   ) _____-_____

Street Address:

_____

City: _____ State: _____ Zip: _____

Dates of Employment: (State, Month, Year)

From: _____ To: _____

Supervisor Name:

_____

Hour or Weekly Salary: (Start to Last)

_____

Job Title:

_____

Job Description:

_____

_____

Reason for Leaving:

_____

_____

May the Employer be Contacted? _____Yes _____No

Employer Name:

_____

Telephone: (   ) _____-_____

Street Address:

_____

City: _____ State: _____ Zip: _____

Dates of Employment: (State, Month, Year)

From: _____ To: _____

Supervisor Name:

_____

Hour or Weekly Salary: (Start to Last)

_____

Job Title:

_____

Job Description:

_____

_____

Reason for Leaving:

_____

_____

May the Employer be Contacted? _____Yes _____No

Military Experience

Have you ever served in the Armed Forces? _____Yes_____No

If you answered yes, in what branch of military did you serve?

From: _____To: _____

Education Received: _____

What was your reason for leaving the Service?

_____

Training/Specialty Received:

_____

_____

Personal References

Please do not use former employees or relatives

Name: _____

Occupation: _____

Street Address:

_____

City:_____State:_____ Zip:_____

Phone number: (Home) (   )_____-_____(Work) (   )_____-_____

Relationship: _____

Name: _____

Occupation: _____

Street Address: _____

City: _____State: _____ Zip: _____

Phone number: (Home) (   ) _____-_____(Work) (   ) _____-_____

Relationship: _____

Name: _____

Occupation: _____

Street Address: _____

City: _____State: _____ Zip: _____

Phone number: (Home) (   ) _____-_____ (Work) (   ) _____-_____

Relationship: _____

Name: _____

Occupation: _____

Street Address: _____

City: _____State: _____ Zip: _____

Phone number: (Home) (   ) _____-_____ (Work) (   ) _____-_____

Relationship: _____

Please use the space provided below to summarize any additional information to help describe your qualifications.

_____

_____

_____

_____

DO IT YOURSELF: Chronological Resume- *This worksheet can be used to help you collect information, and create a proper chronological resume.*

Permanent Address:

Name: _____

Address: _____

City: _____ State: _____ Zip: _____

Phone (Daytime) - (   ) - __ __ __ - __ __ __ __

(Evening) - (   ) - __ __ __ - __ __ __ __

Cell Phone: (   ) __ __ __ - __ __ __ __

Email: _____

Current/Temporary Address:

Name: _____

Address: _____

City: _____ State: _____ Zip: _____

Phone (Daytime) - (   ) - __ __ __ - __ __ __ __

(Evening) - (   ) - __ __ __ - __ __ __ __

**Nicknames are not recommended for use in a chronological resume. If you do not own your own phone, it is okay to provide a phone number where a message can be lift.

** **Summary statement:** This section is similar to an objective statement, but instead of stating your career goals, it provides a brief summary of your relevant experience and qualification. A Summary Statement should be as concise as possible.

EXAMPLE: ""Experienced Pharmacy Technician with over five years of experience in prescription processing, medication dispensing, and customer service. Skilled in accurately interpreting prescription orders, managing inventory, and providing exceptional patient care. Detail-oriented and committed to maintaining a clean, organized, and safe work environment."

- _____

- _____

- _____

Work /Relevant Experience: This section details the qualifications and abilities you possess that would make you an ideal candidate for the position.

* Position Title

EXAMPLE: Pharmacy Technician Supervisor

*Company Name

EXAMPLE: SAS Drug

* City

EXAMPLE: Columbia, State: SC

* Dates of Employment:

EXAMPLE: (Month/Year), From (May, 2004) To (Present)

* Work Description: Specific abilities, duties, and accomplishments should be listed here. Most recent experience should be listed first. Bullet point format should be used as opposed to paragraph format.

EXAMPLE: Trained and supervised a team of 17.

- _____

- _____

- _____

Position Title: _____

Company Name:_____

City: _____ State: _____

Dates of Employment (Month/Year) From: _____ to _____

Work Description:

- _____

- _____

- _____

- _____

Position Title: _____

Company Name:_____

City: _____ State: _____

Dates of Employment (Month/Year) From: _____ to _____

Work Description:

- _____

- _____

- _____

- _____

Education: Your most recent educational degree should be listed first.

Educational Institution: _____

City: _____ State: _____

Dates of Attendance: _____ To_____ (Month/Year)

Major(s): _____

Minor(s): _____

Certificate(s)/Degree (s): _____

GPA: _____/_____ (**EXAMPLE:** 3.75/4.00 GPA. Should only be included if higher than 3.0.)

Educational Institution: _____

City: _____ State: _____

Dates of Attendance: _____ To_____ (Month/Year)

Major(s): _____

Minor(s): _____

Certificate(s)/Degree (s): _____

GPA: _____/_____ (**EXAMPLE:** 3.75/4.00 GPA. Should only be included if higher than 3.0.)

High School/GED: _____

City: _____ State:_____
Year Graduated _____ (*OPTIONAL: Not preferred if you have been out of high school more than three years.*)

College/High School-Related Activities: Can include honors received in high school and college. Leadership activities, membership in clubs/organizations should be included. Activities should be listed with bullet points.

EXAMPLE: President, Allied Health Sciences Society of America

- _____

- _____

- _____

- _____

Members in professional or trade associations, service clubs, community/social organizations, volunteer work, and internships can be listed here. Leadership roles or offices held in any organizations can also be listed, as well as any interests or hobbies.

EXAMPLE: Member, Future Teachers of America

- _____

- _____

- _____

- _____

Key Course Highlights: OPTIONAL. Use this section if you have little work experience, or are seeking a job outside of your field of study. Four-six courses related to your career objective should be listed.

- _____

- _____

- _____

- _____

References: List individuals who know you well and can communicate your character, accomplishments, achievements, work habits, and experiences. Examples of references include teachers, co-workers, present employer, former supervisors, and friends. Four to six references should be listed. You must ask the person's permission to include them as a reference. When pursuing a position, assure that you keep in contact with your references.

Name: _____ J o b Title: _____

Home or Business Address: _____

City: _____ State: _____ Zip: _____

Home Phone (   ) __ __ __ - __ __ __ __

Work Phone (   ) __ __ __ - __ __ __ __

Name: _____ J o b Title: _____

Home or Business Address: _____

City: _____ State: _____ Zip: _____

Home Phone (   ) __ __ __ - __ __ __ __

Work Phone (   ) __ __ __ - __ __ __ __

Name: _____ J o b Title: _____

Home or Business Address: _____

City: _____ State: _____ Zip: _____

Home Phone (   ) __ __ __ - __ __ __ __

Work Phone (   ) __ __ __ - __ __ __ __

Name: _____ J o b Title: _____

Home or Business Address: _____

City: _____ State: _____Zip: _____

Home Phone (   ) __ __ __ - __ __ __ __

Work Phone (   ) __ __ __ - __ __ __ __

Do It Yourself: Functional Resume-*This worksheet can be used to help you collect information, and compose a suitable functional resume.*

Permanent Address:

Name: _____

Street Address: _____

City: _____ State: _____ Zip: _____

Phone (Daytime): (   )-___ ___ ___-___ ___ ___ ___

Phone (Evening): (   )-___ ___ ___-___ ___ ___ ___

Cell Phone: (   )-___ ___ ___-___ ___ ___ ___

Email: _____

Current/Temporary Address:

Name: _____

Street Address: _____

City: _____ State: _____ Zip: _____

Phone (Daytime): (   )-___ ___ ___-___ ___ ___ ___

Phone (Evening): (   )-___ ___ ___-___ ___ ___ ___

Cell Phone: (   )-___ ___ ___-___ ___ ___ ___

**Nicknames are not recommended for use in a functional resume. If you do not own your own phone, it is okay to provide a phone number where a message can be left. **

Career Objective: This category lets the employer know what position you are seeking within the company. An objective statement should be as concise as possible.

EXAMPLE: "Desire a leading role as an advertising representative within the company."

- _____

- _____

- _____

- _____

Summary/Highlights of Qualifications: This section should include three or four abilities that fulfill the needs of the employer. These skills should preferably be listed in bullet format; however, using paragraph form is acceptable.

- _____

- _____

- _____

- _____

Professional or Related Experience: Documentation of specific professional and related skills should be included in this section. Three or four categories should identify the action-oriented statements that are listed.

Possible Categories: EXAMPLE: Supervisor Abilities- General skills should be listed such as technical skills, communication skills, public relation skills, and management skills. Specific action-related skills should also be listed in bullet point form. These statements should explain overall skill areas.

EXAMPLE: Train, schedule, supervise staff of seven.

- _____

- _____

- _____

- _____

Employment History: Most recent work experience should be listed first in this category. Include dates, company, job title, and company location. Volunteer, military, or other career-related activities can also be listed here. It is NOT recommended to include experience beyond a 15-year period UNLESS you currently work for the same company.

EXAMPLE: Date: 1998-Present **Job Title:** Purchasing Manager **Company:** Valley Imports **City and State:** Virginia Beach, Va.

Date: _____ Job Title:_____

Company: _____

City and State: _____

Date: _____ Job Title:_____

Company: _____

City and State: _____

Date: _____ Job Title:_____

Company: _____

City and State: _____

Date: _____ Job Title:_____

Company: _____

City and State: _____

Education: Most recent educational degree should be listed first.

Educational Institution: _____

City: _____ State: _____

Attendance Dates - From: _____To: _____
(Month/Year)

Major(s): _____

Minor(s):
_____

Certificate(s)/Degree(s): _____

G.P.A. _____ (Grade Point Average should
only be listed if it is 3.0 or higher.)

Educational Institution: _____

City: _____ State: _____

Attendance Dates -From: _____To: _____
(Month/Year)

Major(s): _____

Minor(s): _____

Certificate(s)/Degree(s): _____

G.P.A. _____ (Grade Point Average should only be listed if it is 3.0 or higher.)

High School/GED: _____

City: _____ State: _____

Graduation Year _____ (OPTIONAL. Typically, only listed if you have been out of high school three years or less.)

Professional Affiliations: OPTIONAL. Can include memberships to community/social organizations, internships, volunteer work, and professional or trade organizations. Leadership offices or roles should be listed, as well as interests or hobbies.

EXAMPLE: Treasurer of Virginia Association of Retail Management

- _____

- _____

- _____

- _____

References: List individuals who know you well and can communicate your character, accomplishments, achievements, work habits, and experiences. Examples of references include teachers, co-workers, present employer, former supervisors, and friends. Four to six references should be listed. You must ask the person's permission to include them as a reference. When pursuing a position, assure that you keep in contact with your references.

Name: _____ Job Title: _____

Home/Business Address: _____

City: _____ State: _____ Zip: _____

Home Phone: (   )-___ ___ ___ -___ ___ ___ ___

Work Phone: (   )- ___ ___ ___ -___ ___ ___ ___

Name: _____Job Title: _____

Home/Business Address: _____

City: _____ State: _____Zip: _____

Home Phone: (   )-___ ___ ___ -___ ___ ___ ___

Work Phone: (   )- ___ ___ ___ -___ ___ ___ ___

Name: _____ Job Title: _____

Home/Business Address: _____

City: _____ State: _____ Zip: _____

Home Phone: (   )-___ ___ ___-___ ___ ___ ___

Work Phone: (   )-_____-_____

Thank you for your purchase of
Job Seeker's Best Friend:
*The Complete Resume Writing and
Career Guide Book*
by Courtney Miller and Sarah Snypes
of ***Pharm Techs Only!*™**

Although this book was written for all job seekers,
we do provide an online one-stop-shop for career
advancement specifically for pharmacy technicians,
including a job board, social network and all info pharm
tech related.

If you are currently
a pharmacy technician anywhere in the world, or are interested
in the profession, please visit www.pharmtechsonly.com
for endless information.

If you have any questions or comments about the guide book,
please contact us at questions@pharmtechsonly.com.

www.ingramcontent.com/pod-product-compliance
Lightning Source LLC
Chambersburg PA
CBHW081414280526
45788CB00009B/3093